Mental Maths

Daily Workout

Marian Bond

Pearson Education Limited
Edinburgh Gate
Harlow
Essex, CM20 2JE
England

© Pearson Education Limited 1999

ISBN 0582 41006 1

Designed by Ken Vail Graphic Design, Cambridge.

Printed in China.

The publisher's policy is to use paper manufactured from sustainable forests.

Introduction

Mental Maths Daily Workout is a series of books for pupils aged 4–11.

Book R for pupils aged 4–5 in Reception/P 1.

Book 1 for pupils aged 5–6 in Year 1/P 2.

Book 2 for pupils aged 6–7 in Year 2/P 3.

Book 3 for pupils aged 7–8 in Year 3/P 4.

Book 4 for pupils aged 8–9 in Year 4/P 5.

Book 5 for pupils aged 9–10 in Year 5/P 6.

Book 6 for pupils aged 10–11 in Year 6/P 7.

Mental Maths Daily Workout contains two types of mental activities:

■ ORAL maths where the questions and responses are verbal. The ORAL maths sections should be used every day at the beginning of the Numeracy Lesson.

■ MENTAL maths where the questions and answers are written but the calculation should occur in the head. Each copymaster provides one week's written MENTAL maths practice.

ORAL Maths

■ The ORAL maths activities have been designed as a whole class activity.

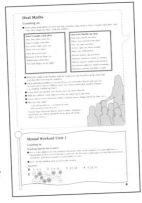

■ Each unit's ORAL activities represent approximately one week's work for approximately 5–10 minutes each time and have a clearly stated purpose.

■ The ORAL activities develop skills independent of that unit's MENTAL activities. Many of the skills are applied later in the MENTAL work.

■ Many of the activities include 'show me' problems where pupils hold up different types of Number Cards in response to the questions. This avoids the problem of some pupils calling out the answer and of others not taking part.

■ Once you have used a particular activity and once the children are familiar with a particular resource, you can continue using it in subsequent weeks alongside the new activities that are introduced in every unit.

■ There is a guide to the resources you will need for the activities on pages 62–64.

MENTAL Maths

■ Each week's MENTAL maths activities have been written in three sets.

■ Pupils can read the questions and write their answers on the copymaster or, alternatively, the questions can be read out orally and pupils can record their answers.

■ The answers to most of the questions are given beneath the Teaching Tips on the non-photocopiable page.

Record Sheets

Two record sheets are provided on pages 60 and 61. The Mental Maths Record Sheet on page 60 provides teachers with a chart for recording the date a particular unit was completed and any appropriate notes. The Mental Maths Pupil's Record Sheet on page 61 allows a pupil to keep a record of the sheets completed and, if required, a score for each set in a unit.

CONTENTS

Oral Maths

Counting on

■ Find a place with plenty of room and sing counting songs such as 'Once I caught a fish alive' and 'One, two, buckle my shoe', with the children.

Once I caught a fish alive

One, two, three, four, five,

Once I caught a fish alive.

Six, seven, eight, nine, ten,

Then I let it go again.

Why did you let it go?

Because it bit my finger so.

Which finger did it bite?

This little finger, on the right!

One two, buckle my shoe

One, two, buckle my shoe.

Three, four, knock at the door.

Five, six, pick up sticks.

Seven, eight, lay them straight.

Nine, ten, a big fat hen.

Eleven, twelve, dig and delve.

Thirteen, fourteen, maids a-courting.

Fifteen, sixteen, maids in the kitchen.

Seventeen, eighteen, maids in waiting.

Nineteen, twenty, my plate's empty.

■ When the children are familiar with the songs you can sing them in the classroom and clap when you sing the numbers.

■ Allow individual children to choose from a set of Number Word Cards one–ten. As each card is selected children carry out a given action that number of times, e.g. clapping, holding up fingers.

■ Count from any number you choose up to no more than 20.

■ With the children, count objects as they are tidied up or put away.

■ Count objects in the classroom (tables, window panes, things which are blue, etc.).

■ Play an 'I Spy' game:

> *'I spy with my little eye… six things the same.*
> *Who can tell me what they are?'*

Choose large classroom objects such as tables, windows, pencil pots, etc. (There should be fewer than 20 of the object you choose.)

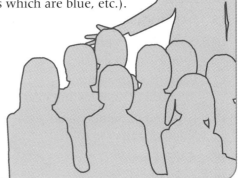

Mental Workout Unit 1

Counting on

Teaching Tips for Set A and C

■ Set A: if the children are not confident about the order of the numbers, let each child have a Numberline 0–20 or a set of Number Cards (see the Resource Guide pages 62–64) laid out in front of him/her. Ask them to point to each number in turn.

■ Set C: let the children look at real or play money.

Answers

A ① 3, 5   ② 7, 9, 11   ③ 17, 18   ④ 9, 12, 13

C

A

Write the missing numbers.

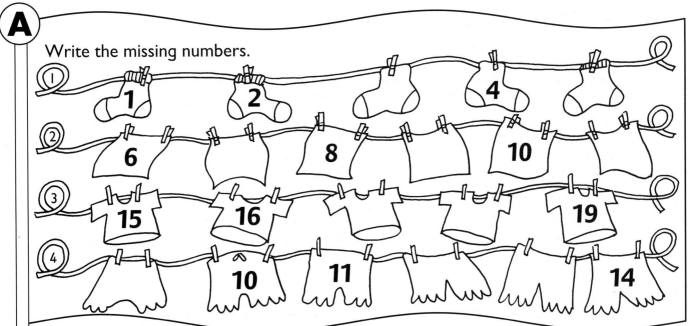

1   2   4

6   8   10

15   16   19

10   11   14

B

Match the words and numbers.

6

eight

two

2

8

six

5

zero

five

0

C

Colour the silver coins.

Oral Maths

Counting back

- Get the children to crouch down and clasp their hands above their heads like a rocket cone. Count down, first from 5, and later from 10, to 0 followed by '*Blast off!*'. (The children 'launch' themselves.)

- Sing songs which involve counting backwards such as, 'Five fat sausages', 'Five little monkeys' and 'Ten green bottles'.

- Show the children numbers on a Numberline (see the Resource Guide pages 62–64). Count back from 5 and then from 10 to 0, clapping as you say each number.

- Count back from any number you choose, not more than 20, to zero.

- Count down from 10 (or 5) as you give the children time to tidy up or get ready for the next activity.

Numberlines

Using a set of Number Cards (see the Resource Guide pages 62–64), to be laid on the floor or pegged to a washing line, carry out the following activities:

- Distribute the cards among the children and invite them to help you assemble the line.

- Ask the children to cover their eyes as you remove a number which they can then identify.

- Swap two numbers around and ask children to spot the change.

- Build the numberline again, adding the numbers in random order. Ask children to place their card on the line and encourage them to explain why they have chosen that particular position, e.g. needing to leave room for other numbers.

Mental Workout Unit 2

Counting back

Teaching Tips for Set A

- Let the children have a Numberline or a set of Number Cards (see the Resource Guide pages 62–64) laid out in front of them if they are not confident with the order of the numbers. Ask them to point to each number in turn.

Answers

A ① 8, 7 ② 2, 0 ③ 18, 17, 15 ④ 13, 12, 9

C ① square ② circle ③ triangle

Unit 2

A

Write the missing numbers.

B

Colour the largest picture in each set.

C

Label each shape. circle   triangle   square

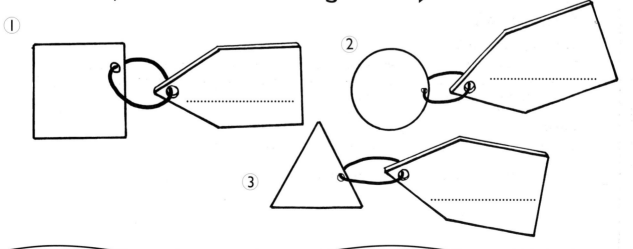

Oral Maths

Counting reliably to 20

■ Using a set of Number Cards (see the Resource Guide pages 62–64) or a whole-class numberline, point to a number and ask a child to collect that number of pencils, building blocks, etc. Count the objects as a class (forwards or backwards) as the child puts them away.

Each child needs a set of Number Cards.

■ Draw a number of objects on the board and ask children to count the objects and hold up the correct Number Card. Encourage children to respond as quickly as they can. Ensure that sometimes the objects are in a recognisable pattern, and sometimes they are arranged at random.

Each child should have an Ele'flip Card (see the Resource Guide pages 62–64).

■ Ask the children to show you a certain number of elephants.

■ Show the children a pattern of elephants on an Ele'flip Card and ask them to show you the same number (not necessarily the same arrangement).

Extending beyond 20

■ Ask children what happens when there are more than 20 objects.
Practise counting beyond 20, reaching 100 as confidence grows.

Mental Workout Unit 3

Match the numbers

Teaching Tips for Set A

■ Ensure the children count just one object for each number named.

Answers

A 7 cats, 5 socks, 12 balls, 15 cars, 10 bananas

B ① 5   ② 12   ③ 17   ④ 20   ⑤ 11   ⑥ 12

C ① Ajit   ② Ajit   ③ Lucy

A

Match the objects to the correct numbers.

10　**15**

8

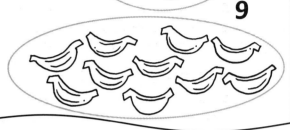

14

7

5

9

10

12

B

Colour the larger number.

①  2　5

②  12　6

③  7　17

④ 20　17

⑤ 4　11

⑥ 12　9

C

Who has more?　Lucy　Ajit

① ....

② ....

③ ....

Oral Maths

In-between

■ Reinforce the meaning of the word 'between' by asking three children to stand in a row. Ask another child to stand between two of them (name which two). Repeat, building up the line of children. You do not have to choose adjacent children for the 'new' child to stand between.

■ Give each child one Number Card from 2 to 19 (see the Resource Guide pages 62–64). Ask all the children to stand. Give instructions such as:

Sit down if your number is between 5 and 12.

(They should only respond if their number is strictly between the given numbers, i.e. 5 and 12 do not sit down.).

Kneel down if your number is between 8 and 17.
Clap if your number is between 7 and 11.

Vary the range of numbers so the children always have to listen to your instruction. Keep the range between 0 and 20.

■ Give some children large Number Cards in a range between and including 0 and 20 (e.g. 7 to 15). Ask two children to stand next to each other. (You do not need to know their numbers before you pick them.) Each of the other children, in turn, chooses where to stand to build up the row of consecutive numbers.

■ Give the children Number Fans (see the Resource Guide pages 62–64). Ask them to hold up a number that is in a certain range, e.g.

Hold up a number between 5 and 8.

■ Play the game 'I am thinking of a number'. Choose a number then say:

I am thinking of a number between 0 and 20.

The children are allowed to ask questions to discover your number but you will only answer yes or no. Encourage children to appreciate that the best questions are those that eliminate the most numbers, e.g. *Is it bigger than 10?* is a good question because it eliminates half the numbers.

Mental Workout Unit 4

Add 1, 2 or 3

Teaching Tips for Set A

■ Each child should have a Numberline 0–20 (see the Resource Guide pages 62–64). When the children use the line to count, on ensure that they are matching one movement to one count.

Answers

A ① 17   ② 15   ③ 19   ④ 11   ⑤ 20   ⑥ 14

B ① 4   ④ 9   **C**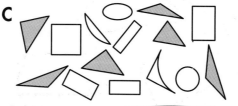
　　② 3   ⑤ 10
　　③ 6   ⑥ 15

Name   Class

A

Write the answers.

① 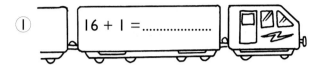 16 + 1 = ...

④  10 + 1 = ...

② 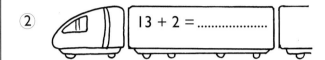 13 + 2 = ...

⑤ 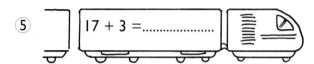 17 + 3 = ...

③  18 + 1 = ...

⑥  12 + 2 = ...

B

Colour the smaller number.

①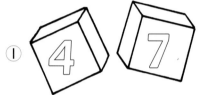

④

②

⑤

③

⑥

C

Colour the triangles.

Oral Maths

Counting in twos

Stand the children in a circle.

■ The first child stamps one foot then the other, counting 1, 2. The second child takes up the count 3, 4, and so on around the circle.

■ Play the game again but this time each child only says the number that goes with the second stamp. (The first number can be whispered.)

Write the numbers 1 to 20 in order on the board. With the class read *every other* number and as you say it mark it in some way (e.g. put a ring around it).

■ Read the marked numbers with the class.

■ Starting with 2, ask each child in turn to read one number in the sequence up to 20. (When you reach 20 start again at 2 until every child has said one number.)

■ Repeat the activity with the children counting down in twos from 20 to 0.

■ Ask the children, as a class or individually, to count on or back in twos from any even number you choose (between 0 and 20).

Mental Workout Unit 5

Subtract 1, 2 or 3

Teaching Tips for Set A and C

■ Set A: each child should have a Numberline 0–20 (see the Resource Guide pages 62–64). When the children count back, ensure that they match one movement to one count.

■ Set C: let the children use real or play money.

Answers

A ① 15   ③ 16   ⑤ 8

    ② 11   ④ 11   ⑥ 18

B It is not specified whether the order should be counting order or reverse order, so accept both and discuss the different possibilities with the class, group or child.

C Accept 10p and any combination of 5p, 2p and 1p coins that add up to 10p.

Unit 5

A

Write the answers.

①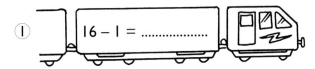
16 – 1 = ...

④
12 – 1 = ...

②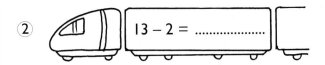
13 – 2 = ...

⑤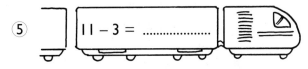
11 – 3 = ...

③
19 – 3 = ...

⑥
20 – 2 = ...

B

Write the numbers in order.

①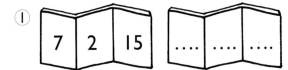
7   2   15   ....

④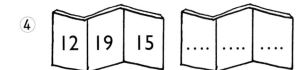
12   19   15   ....

②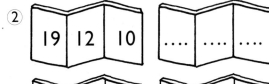
19   12   10   ....

⑤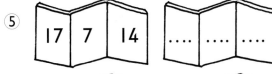
17   7   14   ....

③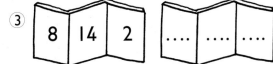
8   14   2   ....

⑥
1   19   11   ....

C

Draw three different ways to make 10p.

①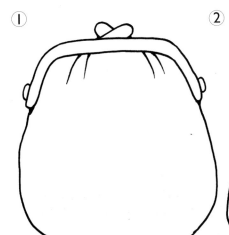

②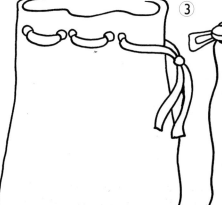

③

Oral Maths

Odd and even

- Write the numbers 1 to 10 and 11 to 20 in two rows, one above the other, or use a 100-square.
- Ask the children to show you the numbers they would say when counting in twos. Look at the numbers they have indicated and ask them to continue the sequence.
- Ask what you are counting on by in each case. (2)
- Look for the patterns produced by the numbers. (Every marked number ends with digits 2, 4, 6, 8, or 0.)
- Ask individual children to choose one of these numbers and count out that number of bricks. Can they share their bricks fairly with a friend? Repeat this activity using the numbers which were not marked. What do the children notice? Explain to the children that those numbers which can be shared fairly between two are called the *even* numbers. Those that cannot be shared fairly between two are called *odd* numbers.

Once children are familiar with the number pattern of the units digits in odd and even numbers play these games:

- Explain to the children that when you say an odd number they are going to sit down, and when you say an even number they are going to stand up. Children will enjoy listening to long numbers such as 'twenty-eight million, three hundred and forty-eight thousand, two hundred and ... four' as they wait for the final digit.
- Build agility by asking individual children to respond to odd or even numbers in the same way. Move around the class as quickly as you can.

Mental Workout Unit 6

Counting objects

Teaching Tips for Set A

- Encourage the children to cross through each item as they count. More able children can be encouraged to pair objects by putting a ring around them in order to count in twos. Talk about how any remaining objects indicate that this is an odd number.

Answers

A ① 10 apples   ② 13 cats   ③ 17 bananas   ④ 20 socks

C ① 2p   ③ 3p   ⑤ 50p

   ② 1p   ④ 20p   ⑥ 11p

| Name | Class | # Unit 6 |

A

How many?

①

③

....

②

④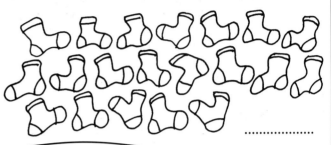

....

....

B

Link the numbers and words.

7   seven

nineteen

eleven   **16**

19

13   **11**

thirteen   sixteen

C

How much money?

①

....

③

....

⑤

....

②

....

④

....

⑥

....

Oral Maths

Doubles to 6

- Ask the children to hold up 4 fingers. Then ask them to make the same number on the other hand. *How many fingers altogether?*

- Draw circles or spots on the board. *How many can you see?* Hold a mirror next to the spots or circles. *How many can you see now?* (Make sure both halves of the class can see the effect by holding the mirror on the 'other side' of the circles too.)

- Each child needs a Number Fan (see the Resource Guide pages 62–64). Call out numbers to 6 and ask children to show you double the number called.

- Do 'double doubles' with starting numbers 1–3, calling out the number and asking the children to show you double the number called, and then double the number shown.

Halving to 12

- Count out 12 children and ask them to stand up. Say that half of them are going to sit down. Ask: *How many should sit down?* Discuss this with the children. Repeat with 6, halving the number of children who are still standing.

- Ask the children to show you a given even number of fingers and then to put half of them down.

- Each child needs a Number Fan. Call out even numbers to 12 and ask children to show you half the number called.

Mental Workout Unit 7

Odd and even

Teaching Tips for Set A and C

- Set A: remind the children about previous experiences with odd and even numbers.

- Set C: if necessary, remind the children that a rectangle has four straight sides and all the corners are like the corners of a page (right angles).

Answers

A
1. 8 10 12
2. 7 9 11
3. 16 18 20
4. 15 17 19
5. 14 12 10

C (A square is a special rectangle and should be included.)

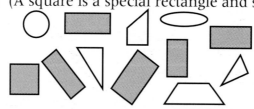

Name	Class

A

Finish the patterns.

①  2 4 6

②  1 3 5

③  10 12 14

④  9 11 13

⑤  20 18 16

B

Complete the sets.

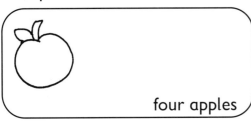

four apples

seven socks

three fish

five cars

C

Colour the rectangles.

Oral Maths

Estimating

■ Draw a number of spots on the board (up to 20) and cover them over with a cloth or a piece of paper. Explain to the children that they are going to estimate the number. Explain that making an estimate is a 'thinking' guess. Uncover the spots for a few seconds (not long enough for the children to count them). Record their estimates on the board. Invite one child to make an actual count.

■ Repeat this activity using real objects, such as pencils or bricks, spread out where the children can see them, inviting estimates from individual children. Discourage counting by asking for quick responses.

■ Ask children to estimate how many times they can jump up and down in one minute, or how many bricks they can stack before a tower collapses.

■ Sit the children in a circle and place a number of objects (up to 20) on a tray, covering the tray with a cloth. Using Number Fans (see the Resource Guide pages 62–64) the children show you their estimate of the number of objects after you have removed the cover for a few seconds and replaced it (remember not to include 11 when you are working with Number Fans).

Mental Workout Unit 8

Add or subtract 2

Teaching Tips for Set A

■ Provide Numberlines or counters to suport less able children.

Answers

A
- ① 7
- ② 5
- ③ 14
- ④ 13
- ⑤ 15
- ⑥ 9
- ⑦ 17
- ⑧ 11

C
- ① 4
- ② 4
- ③ 10
- ④ 12
- ⑤ 5
- ⑥ 8
- ⑦ 5
- ⑧ 2
- ⑨ 6

A

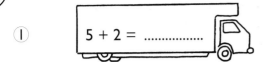
① $5 + 2 =$ ....

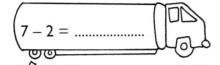
② $7 - 2 =$ ....

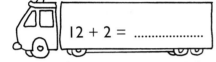
③ $12 + 2 =$ ....

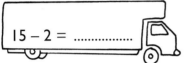
④ $15 - 2 =$ ....

⑤ $13 + 2 =$ ....

⑥ $11 - 2 =$ ....

⑦ $19 - 2 =$ ....

⑧ $9 + 2 =$ ....

B

Tick the line which is longer.

①

②

③

Tick the shorter line.

④

⑤

⑥

C

What is the score?

①  $=$ ......

②  $=$ ......

③ $=$ ......

④  $=$ ......

⑤ $=$ ......

⑥ $=$ ......

⑦  $=$ ......

⑧ $=$ ......

⑨  $=$ ......

Oral Maths

Counting on and back within 20

Mark out a large Numberline (0–20) on a large strip of paper or on the playground.

Cover the faces of a dice with operation symbols: three plus and three minus signs. You will also need a second dice labelled 1, 1, 2, 2, 3, 3.

■ Invite a child to stand on a number towards the middle of the line. Roll the two dice and talk about the operation generated. Discuss with the children whether the standing child should move forwards or backwards. Encourage predictions about the number he/she will land on.

Give the children Number Fans (see the Resource Guide pages 62–64).

■ Using a Numberline 0–20 (see the Resource Guide pages 62–64), point to a number and ask questions such as:

What number is one more than this?
What is one less?
What is two less?
(Be aware that the children cannot show you 11.)

■ Repeat the activity without the Numberline, giving all instructions verbally, e.g.:

What is 1 less than 13?
What is 3 less than 14?

Turning addition sentences around

■ On the board write the sum 1 + 9 = . Using the floor Numberline as above, ask a child to start on number 1 and take 9 steps. *What is the answer to the sum?*

Now start with another child on number 9 and ask her to take 1 step. *Are the children on the same number? Is the answer the same? Which was easier?* Draw the children's attention to the fact that sometimes difficult addition sums can be made easier by turning them around, looking at the larger number first.

■ Using large Number Cards (1–10) (see the Resource Guide pages 62–64), invite individual children to choose two cards. Show them to the class. Ask the choosers to decide which would be the easier way to add the two numbers. Does the class agree?

■ Sit the children in a circle and pass around one dice labelled 1 to 6 and one labelled 7 to 12. Roll the two dice and discuss, as before, the easier way to add the numbers.

Mental Workout Unit 9

Add or subtract 1, 2 or 3

Teaching Tips for Set A

■ Provide Numberlines (see the Resource Guide pages 62–64) or counters to support less able children. Remind the children that additions can be turned around to make the adding easier.

Answers

A ① 6   ③ 15   ⑤ 18   ⑦ 12
    ② 17   ④ 17   ⑥ 17   ⑧ 9

B The children may choose the adjacent numbers, but any numbers which satisfy the conditions are equally acceptable.

C If correctly coloured the picture will reveal a cat.

Name	Class	# Unit 9

A Write the answers.

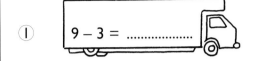

① 9 − 3 = ...

⑤ 2 + 16 = ...

② 15 + 2 = ...

⑥ 20 − 3 = ...

③ 17 − 2 = ...

⑦ 1 + 11 = ...

④ 3 + 14 = ...

⑧ 11 − 2 = ...

B

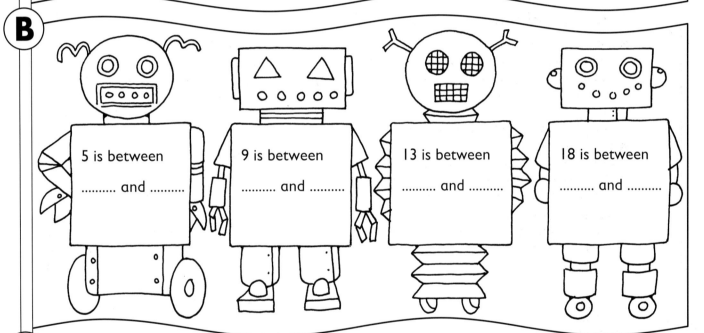

5 is between .... and ....

9 is between .... and ....

13 is between .... and ....

18 is between .... and ....

C

Colour the odd numbers blue. Colour the even numbers red.

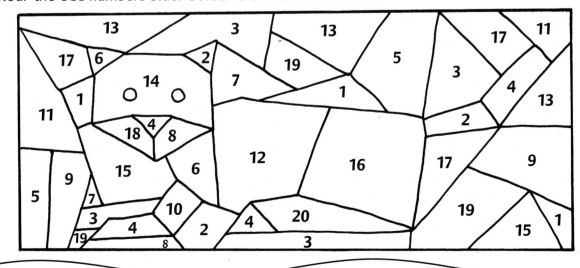

Oral Maths

Counting in tens

Revisit numbers to 100 by counting. Draw attention to nines as a signal of change, e.g. 29, 30; ... 59, 60.

■ Sit the children in a circle. Count around the circle. Each time a number in the family of 10 is said that child jumps up and claps. Carry on counting round and round the circle.

■ Write the numbers 1 to 60 in rows of 10 (1–10, 11–20, 21–30, etc.) on the board, or use a 100-square to show the pattern of counting in tens, 10, 20, 30, etc., each time showing 10 with your hands. Ask the children to count in tens:

Count in tens up to 100, starting from 30 (or any ten you choose).

Count down to 0 in tens, starting from 60 (or any ten you choose).

■ Let the children see a 100-square (with the tens marked or unmarked) as a reference. Ask questions such as:

How many tens do you count from 0 to 40?

How many tens do you count from 20 to 50?

Ask questions about counting backwards as well as forwards.

Mental Workout Unit 10

Counting in ones, twos and tens

Teaching Tips for Set A, B and C

■ Set A: allow the children to see a Numberline.
■ Set B and C: provide reading support.

Answers

A ① 8 9   ③ 30 40   ⑤ 60 50   **B** ① 11   ③ 10
   ② 6 8   ④ 16 14   ⑥ 10 12   ② 13   ④ 10

C ①   ②   ③   ④

Name   Class

A

Write the missing numbers.

① 6 7 _ _ 10

② 2 4 _ _ 10

③ 20 _ _ 50 60

④ 20 18 _ _ 12

⑤ 80 70 _ _ 40

⑥ _ _ 14 16 18

B

① 16 take away 5 is ....

② 17 take away 4 is ....

③ 11 take away 1 is ....

④ 20 take away 10 is ....

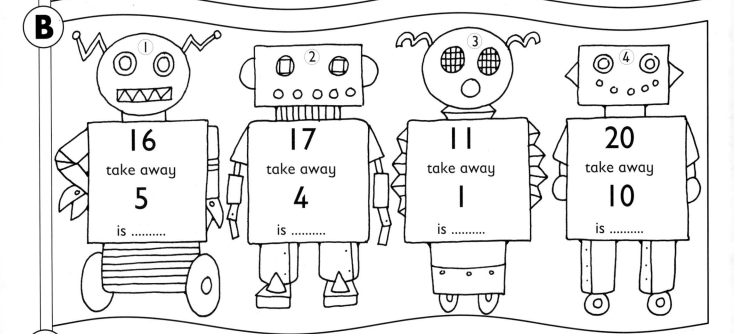

C

Which picture is next?   Tick the correct picture.

① ▭ ▯ ▭ ....   ▯ ▭ ◇

② ▽ △ ▽ ....   △ ▽ ▷

③ ○○ ○○ ○○ ○○ ....   ○○ ○○ ○●
   ● ● ● ●   ● ●   ○

④ B ƍ B ....   B ƍ ꓭ

Oral Maths

Partitioning teens

■ Make a large hoop on the floor using a skipping rope. Explain that this is a space for a set of 10 children. Ask a number of children (between 11 and 20) to stand up. Count the children together and record the number. Now ask 10 of the children to stand in the hoop. How many are standing outside? Repeat for other numbers, each time referring back to the original count. Point out that a 'teen' number is one set of 10 and some more.

■ Use a 100-square or write out the numbers 1 to 10 and 11 to 20 in two rows, one above the other. Start with 9 and add 10 to it. Discuss the pattern of the two numbers (both end with 9). Continue with 8 plus 10 etc.

■ Give each child a set of Digit Cards (see the Resource Guide pages 62–64). Ask the children addition and subtraction questions which involve making teens from '10 plus something', or 10 by subtracting a number (e.g. 15–5). Include questions which involve 11, 12 and 20.

Daily Workout Unit 11

Add or subtract?

Teaching Tips for Set A, B and C

■ Set A: explain to the children that they need to insert the appropriate operation symbol in each of the boxes.

■ Set B and C: provide reading support for less able children as appropriate.

Answers

A ① + ② – ③ – ④ + ⑤ – ⑥ +

Show the children that a number gets bigger if you add to it, and smaller if you take away from it.

B ① odd ② even ③ odd ④ odd ⑤ even

C ① 3 ② 6 ③ no ④ 6

A Add or take away?

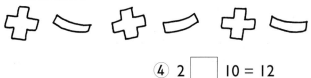

① 6 ☐ 2 = 8

④ 2 ☐ 10 = 12

② 13 ☐ 3 = 10

⑤ 19 ☐ 10 = 9

③ 15 ☐ 2 = 13

⑥ 11 ☐ 4 = 15

B Odd or even?

① five is an .... number

③ three is an .... number

② twenty is an .... number

④ seventeen is an .... number

⑤ eight is an .... number

C

	pig	dog	cat	cow	duck
6					duck
5					duck
4			cat		duck
3	pig		cat	cow	duck
2	pig	dog	cat	cow	duck
1	pig	dog	cat	cow	duck

① How many pigs?

....

② How many ducks?

....

③ Are there fewer cats than cows?

....

④ How many cats and dogs altogether?

....

Oral Maths

Number machines

Make a paper party hat for each child. Mark some of the hats with numbers 0–20 and some with addition or subtraction signs.

■ Ask two children with hats labelled + and 1 to stand at the front of the class holding hands. Explain to the class that these children are a 'number machine' and that they will add 1 to any number. Allow children to suggest numbers to put into the machine and encourage the two machine children to decide together what their output will be. Repeat using different combinations of children to make the machines.

■ Make a number machine using children labelled + and 10. How quickly do children learn to predict the output numbers? Ensure that some of the input numbers are larger than 10. Provide a Numberline to 30 as support.

■ Use the machine 'in reverse'. Provide the output number and ask the children which number must have been the input.

Lazy machines

■ Make a double number machine using four children wearing hats labelled +, 5, – and 5. What do children notice about the pattern of input and output numbers?

■ Change the number that is added and subtracted (e.g. 4 and 4). Can the children predict the result?

Mental Workout Unit 12

Addition within 20

Teaching Tips for Set A and C

■ Set A: encourage the children to use place values, e.g. $12 + 3 = 10 + 2 + 3 = 10 + 5 = 15$ or to partition the numbers into '5 plus something' and then recombine, e.g. $8 + 6 = 5 + 3 + 5 + 1 = 10 + 4 = 14$

■ Set C: ensure that children do not colour half of each individual animal in each set.

Answers

A ① 15   ③ 17   ⑤ 12   ⑦ 13
    ② 19   ④ 20   ⑥ 13   ⑧ 15

C Children should colour 2 elephants, 5 rabbits, 6 butterflies and 4 mice.

A

Write the answers.

① 3 + 12 = ...   ⑤ 7 + 5 = ...

② 17 + 2 = ...   ⑥ 5 + 8 = ...

③ 11 + 6 = ...   ⑦ 6 + 7 = ...

④ 5 + 15 = ...   ⑧ 7 + 8 = ...

B

Write in numbers.

① fifteen ....   ⑤ eighteen ....

② sixteen ....   ⑥ thirteen ....

③ fourteen ....   ⑦ twelve ....

④ twenty ....   ⑧ seventeen ....

C

Colour half the animals in each set.

Oral Maths

Counting in fives

■ Stand the children in a circle.

■ Introduce a rhythmic counting pattern of five beats, such as 'stamp, stamp, clap, clap, jump'. As the children perform the actions, count together to 20. Extend this activity to thinking rather than saying all the numbers except those with a jump.

Write the 'jumping numbers' down on the board. Encourage the children to look for patterns. They should see that all the numbers said when counting in fives end in 0 or 5.

■ Ask the children to find the 'fives' (multiples of five) on a Numberline (0–100) (see the Resource Guide pages 62–64). Ask them to read the 'fives', 5, 10, 15, 20, etc., while they point to the numbers on an individual Numberline, or you point to them on a class Numberline.

■ As a class count in fives to 100 and back to 0.

■ Roll a dice and ask the class or individual children to count that many fives. They can check them off with their fingers, by clapping or by making tally marks. (E.g. the dice shows 3 and the children count '5, 10, 15'.)

Mental Workout Unit 13

Counting money

Teaching Tips for Set A

■ Encourage the children to group similar coins together, i.e. count in 10s, 5s, 2s or 1s and add the results. Provide real or play money if necessary.

Answers

A ① 6p   ③ 40p   ⑤ 17p
      ② 20p   ④ 6p   ⑥ 24p

B ① add   ④ take away
      ② take away   ⑤ take away
      ③ add   ⑥ add

C
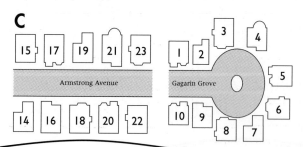

A

How much money?

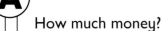

① ....

④ ....

② ....

⑤ ....

③ ....

⑥ ....

B

Add or take away?

➕ ➖ ➕ ➖ ➕ ➖ ➕ ➖ ➕ ➖ ➕ ➖ ➕ ➖ ➕ ➖ ➕ ➖ ➕

➖ ① seven .... two is nine ➖

➕ ② eighteen .... one is seventeen ➕

➖ ③ six .... ten is sixteen ➖

➕ ④ thirteen .... three is ten ➕

➖ ⑤ two .... two is zero ➖

➕ ⑥ five .... five is ten ➕

➖ ➕ ➖ ➕ ➖ ➕ ➖ ➕ ➖ ➕ ➖ ➕ ➖ ➕ ➖ ➕ ➖ ➕ ➖

C

Write the missing house numbers.

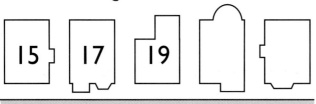

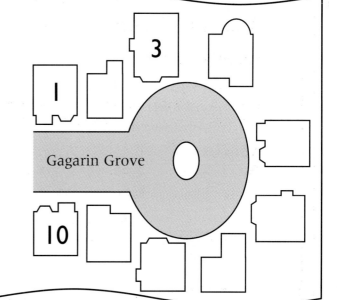

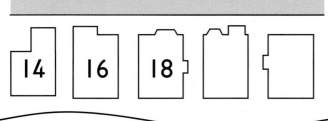

Oral Maths

Changing number sentences

■ Write the numbers 5, 6 and 11 on the board.
  Ask the children to use these numbers to make an addition sum and to tell you their ideas.
  Encourage as wide a variety of language as possible, recording their ideas and suggesting others:

  *5 add 6 makes 11, 5 plus 6 equals 11, 5 and 6 more makes 11, 5 and 6 all together make 11,
  the total of 5 and 6 is 11, the sum of 5 and 6 is 11, etc.*

Now invite the children to use the same numbers to make a subtraction. Again, encourage as wide a
variety of language as possible, again recording ideas:

  *11 take away 5 is 6, 11 take away 6 is 5, 11 subtract 5 is 6, the difference between 6 and 11 is 5,
  11 count back 5 is 6, 6 is 5 less than 11, etc.*

■ Repeat the activity using two dice to generate numbers with which to work.

■ After working on an initial example, the children could be organised into two teams with points
  awarded for each new addition and subtraction sentence.

Mental Workout Unit 14

Number pairs to 4

Teaching Tips for Set A and C

■ Set A: encourage the children to work quickly using number pairs. Provide counters as support.
■ Set C: remind the children of the properties of triangles and rectangles.

Answers

A   ① 3   ③ 4   ⑤ 4   ⑦ 2
     ② 1   ④ 1   ⑥ 3   ⑧ 2

B   ① 8   ③ 15   ⑤ 10
     ② 13   ④ 6   ⑥ 0

C   ① A C F G H   ③ A C F G (because squares are special rectangles)
     ② D E

A

Write the missing numbers.

① 1 + 2 = ...

② 4 − 3 = ...

③ 0 + 4 = ...

④ 3 − 2 = ...

⑤ 2 + 2 = ...

⑥ 4 − 1 = ...

⑦ 2 − 0 = ...

⑧ 3 − 1 = ...

B

① The total of 5 and 3 is ....

② The total of 9 and 4 is ....

③ The total of 10 and 5 is ....

④ 9 subtract 3 is ....

⑤ 14 subtract 4 is ....

⑥ 1 subtract 1 is ....

C

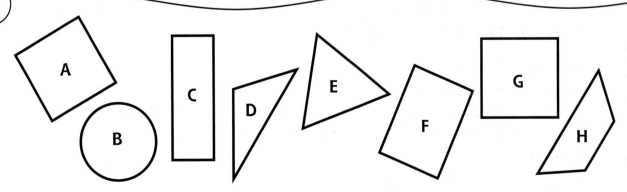

① Which shapes have four sides? ....

② Which shapes are triangles? ....

③ Which shapes are rectangles? ....

Oral Maths

Doubles and near doubles

Give each child a Number Card (1–6) (ensure there is an even number of each digit) (see the Resource Guide pages 62–64).

- Ask the children to find a partner who has the same number.
- Ask them to say what 'their total' is. Ask the children to sit in their pairs facing each other and in order from 1 to 6. Talk about doubles.
- Get the children to look to see who is *near* them (i.e. on their left and right). Discuss the totals they make with their near partners. Discuss what near partners 1 and 6 would have if more numbers were available. Talk about 'near doubles'.
- Ask the children to separate and spread out. Now ask them to find a near double and sit down together. (It doesn't have to be the same person they were sitting next to.) You will have some children who cannot find a partner. Each of these children has to approach a pair, check they are a near double and give the total.
- Call out a total (a result of a double or a near double). The children have to find a partner to make the total with. Decide whether to include other combinations (e.g. if you call '6', is only 3 and 3 allowed or will you include 4 and 2 and 5 and 1 and discuss whether they are doubles, near doubles or not?).

Find all the 'doubles' in a set of dominoes. Record the total number of spots for each one.

- Find the dominoes which are near doubles. Discuss how they may be thought of in two ways (e.g. 4 and 5 is one more than double 4 or one less than double 5).
- Using double and near double dominoes only, ask the children to find certain totals.

- Give the children Number Fans or sets of Number Cards (see the Resource Guide pages 62–64).
- Give them an addition of doubles or near doubles and ask them for the total.
- Ask them for the numbers required to give you doubles and near doubles e.g. 12 needs 6 and 6, 13 needs 6 and 7.

  In each case ask children to talk about how they worked out their answer.

Mental Workout Unit 15

Subtraction by counting back

Teaching Tips for Set A and B

- Set A: some children may need help with the last three questions. Allow a Numberline if necessary.
- Set B: explain to the children how to perform the same operation with each input number. Allow a Numberline if necessary.

Answers

A ① 2 ③ 5 ⑤ 8 ⑦ 2
    ② 16 ④ 13 ⑥ 3 ⑧ 4

B ① 4 ③ 11 ⑤ 6 ⑦ 14 **C** ① 12 ③ 6 ⑤ 11
    ② 8 ④ 20 ⑥ 9 ⑧ 18   ② 9 ④ 3 ⑥ 8

A

Which number is ◇ ?

① 6 – 4 = ◇ .... ⑤ 12 – 4 = ◇ ....

② 19 – 3 = ◇ .... ⑥ 8 – ◇ = 5 ....

③ 11 – 6 = ◇ .... ⑦ 13 – ◇ = 11 ....

④ 18 – 5 = ◇ .... ⑧ 12 – ◇ = 8 ....

B

① 2 | add two | .... ⑤ 2 | add four | ....

② 6 | add two | .... ⑥ 5 | add four | ....

③ 9 | add two | .... ⑦ 10 | add four | ....

④ 18 | add two | .... ⑧ 14 | add four | ....

C

How many spots?

① 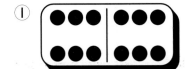 .... ④ 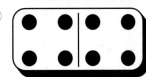 ....

② .... ⑤ ....

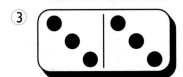

③ .... ⑥ ....

Oral Maths

Number pairs for 5

Each child should have five counters and a sheet or card divided into two halves. Put all the counters on the left of the sheet and ask how many counters there are.

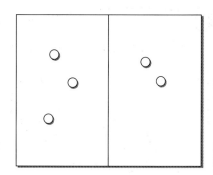

- Find and record all the number pairs for five.
- Ask questions involving the number pairs for five.
- Show the children five small objects. Hide some in your hand and put the rest on the table. Ask how many are hidden in your hand. Repeat the game until the children can answer quickly.

Number pairs for 10

- Stand 10 children in a row. Explain that after a count of 5 each child is going to choose whether they stand up or sit down. In each case record the numbers sitting and standing as addition sums with an answer of 10.

  Who can see any other sums that would also make 10?

- Clap a number between 1 and 10 and ask the children to slowly clap back the number needed to make 10.

- Each child needs an Ele'flip Card (see the Resource Guide pages 62–64). Call out numbers and ask the children to show the number needed to make 10. Alternatively you could show a number with another Ele'flip Card.

Mental Workout Unit 16

Addition and subtraction within 20

Teaching Tips for Set A and B

- Set A: revise all of the techniques learnt so far for addition and subtraction. Ask 'word problems' as well as plain 'number questions'.
- Set B: include thumbs, encourage the children to count in 5s.

Answers

A　①10　　③3　　⑤17
　　②16　　④13　　⑥12

B　①15　　③30　　⑤40
　　②35　　④50

A Join each sum to its answer.

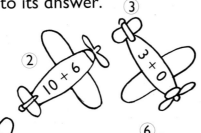

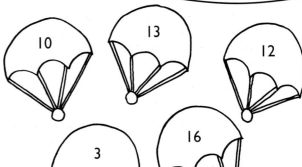
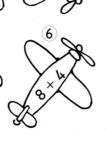

B How many fingers?

1 ....
2 ....
3 ....
4 ....
5 ....

C Continue the patterns.

1   1 (2) 3 (4) 5 (6) 7 (8) 9 10 11 12 13 14 15 16 17 18 19 20

2   (1) 2 (3) 4 (5) 6 (7) 8 9 10 11 12 13 14 15 16 17 18 19 20

3   1 2 (3) 4 5 (6) 7 8 (9) 10 11 12 13 14 15 16 17 18 19 20

4   1 2 3 (4) 5 6 7 (8) 9 10 11 (12) 13 14 15 16 17 18 19 20

5   (5) 6 7 8 9 (10) 11 12 13 14 (15) 16 17 18 19 20 21 22 23 24 25 26

Oral Maths

Patterns with addition

■ Look at a number pattern such as: $10 + 2 = 12$

$$11 + 2 = 13$$
$$12 + 2 = 14$$
$$13 + 2 = 15, \text{ etc.}$$

Discuss what is happening to the first number and to the 'answer' and why. (You start each 'sentence' with 1 more, so you will end with 1 more, as each time you are adding the same amount.)

Investigate similar patterns:

■ Start with the same number and each time add 1 more.

■ Reduce each starting number by 1 and increase each adding number by 1 (same answer each time).

■ Revise the addition pattern of number bonds to 10, pairing up bonds with the same numbers in a different order e.g. $4 + 6 = 10$ $6 + 4 = 10$.

■ Use apparatus to explore the patterns, e.g. manipulating objects, money, building towers of blocks, etc.

■ Show how the patterns can be seen on a Numberline.

Revision of doubles and near doubles

Give each child a set of Number Cards (1–12) (see the Resource Guide pages 62–64).

■ Use two sets of Dice Cards (see the Resource Guide pages 62–64) as 'flash cards' to show 'double scores' (e.g. 4 and 4) from two dice. Ask the children to hold up the total score.

■ Use Dice Cards and large Number Cards to show the children pairs of 'near doubles'. Ask the children to hold up the total score.

■ Give the children a score and ask them for half of it.

■ Give the children a score and the number on one dice, and ask them for the other number (all doubles or near doubles).

■ Repeat the activity orally, without the cards as reference.

Mental Workout Unit 17

Doubles and near doubles

Teaching Tips for Set A

■ Encourage the children to work quickly as they use doubles and near doubles to find the answers.

Answers

A ① 10	③ 12	⑤ 9	⑦ 5	⑨ 7
② 6	④ 4	⑥ 11	⑧ 8	⑩ 11

B ① 2	③ 8	⑤ 12	⑦ 16	**C**
② 5	④ 11	⑥ 15	⑧ 18	

A

Write the answers.

1) 5 + 5 = ...

2) 3 + 3 = ...

3) 6 + 6 = ...

4) 2 + 2 = ...

5) 4 + 5 = ...

6) 6 + 5 = ...

7) 2 + 3 = ...

8) 4 + 4 = ...

9) 3 + 4 = ...

10) 5 + 6 = ...

B

Write the answers.

1) 6 (take away four) ....

2) 9 (take away four) ....

3) 12 (take away four) ....

4) 15 (take away four) ....

5) 2 (add ten) ....

6) 5 (add ten) ....

7) 6 (add ten) ....

8) 8 (add ten) ....

C

Write the even numbers in the square.
Write the odd numbers in the triangle.

12   5   26   19   3   10   21   7   24   18   30

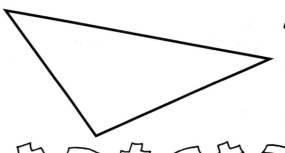

Oral Maths

Revision of number pairs for 10

- Give each child a Number Strip (see the Resource Guide pages 62–64). Either give them ten counters so they can mark up to ten of the sections or give them a rubber band or paperclip to mark a dividing line on the strip.

- Ask the children to cover or separate four divisions on the left of the strip. Ask them how many sections are unmarked or are to the right of the divider. Work methodically, starting with one counter or separating one section, up to ten counters. Ask the children to predict how many sections will be left if they mark or separate a certain number.

- Say a number and ask the children to hold up the required amount of fingers to make ten (e.g. you say '3' and they hold up 7 fingers), or ask them to show you the number on a Number Fan (see the Resource Guide pages 62–64).

Number pairs for 20

- Make a string of 20 beads. Invite individuals to take it in turns to separate the beads along the string to make two sets. Record the number of beads in each set. Can the children spot any missing pairs?

- Extend by asking the children to find the matching pairs of number bonds.

- Compare the results with the number bonds to 10. Encourage children to see that knowing the bonds to 10 can help them work out the bonds from 11 to 20, e.g. 6 + 4 = 10 and 16 + 4 = 20.

- Call out numbers between 11 and 20 and ask the children to show you using Number Fans (see the Resource Guide pages 62–64) the number needed to make 20.

Mental Workout Unit 18

Addition of three numbers

Teaching Tips for Set A

- Children will need Numberlines (see the Resource Guide pages 62–64) and counters to support them, because they are adding three different numbers together. Encourage the children to look for efficient ways of adding the numbers, e.g. look for doubles or tens, start with the largest, etc.

Answers

A   (1) 8   (3) 18   (5) 9   (7) 15
    (2) 10   (4) 10   (6) 17   (8) 20

B   (1) 9   (3) 10   (5) 10   (7) 18
    (2) 7   (4) 7   (6) 18   (8) 6

Unit 18

A

① 5 + 1 + 2 = ...

② 6 + 2 + 2 = ...

③ 7 + 10 + 1 = ...

④ 3 + 5 + 2 = ...

⑤ 6 + 2 + 1 = ...

⑥ 10 + 5 + 2 = ...

⑦ 3 + 6 + 6 = ...

⑧ 10 + 9 + 1 = ...

B

① ....

② ....

③ ....

④ ....

⑤ ....

⑥ ....

⑦ ....

⑧ ....

add one

subtract one

subtract two

add two

ten more

take away one

add ten

two more

8

C

Match the shapes to their names.

cone

cube

cylinder

cuboid

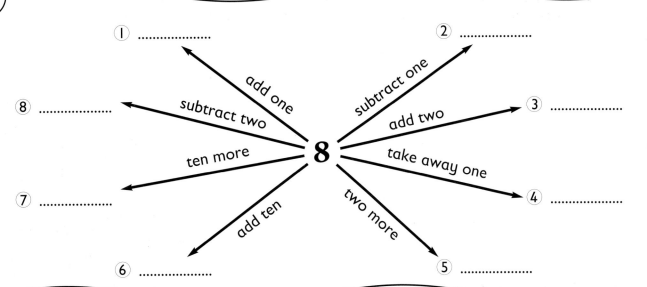

Oral Maths

Add 11 and 9

Each child needs a Number Fan or Digit Cards (see the Resource Guide pages 62–64).

■ Practise adding 10 to any one-digit number by calling out numbers and asking the children to show the answers on their Number Fans.

■ Now explain to the children that you are going to practice adding 11. What can the children tell you about the number 11? (11 is 1 more than 10.) Show how you can add 11 by adding 10 and then adding 1 more. Let the children practise adding 11 to any one-digit number, using their Number Fans to show the answer.

■ Explain that we can use a similar idea to help us add 9.

Ask for the connection between 10 and 9. (9 is one less than 10.) Ask for a quick way of adding 9 to a number. (Add 10 and take 1 away.) Let the children practise adding 9 to a one-digit number, using their Number Fans as before.

Mental Workout Unit 19

Difference between

Teaching Tips for Set A and C

■ Set A: remind the children that finding a difference is the same as subtracting the smaller number from the larger, counting on from the smaller to the larger or counting back from the larger to the smaller.

■ Set C: explain to children that they can use only the coins shown and that no change is given.

Answers

A ① 2   ③ 7   ⑤ 2   ⑦ 5
   ② 5   ④ 10   ⑥ 3   ⑧ 10

C   They can buy the sweets for 3p, 4p, 11p or 13p.

A

Find the difference between these numbers.

① 6 and 4   ....

② 2 and 7   ....

③ 10 and 3   ....

④ 4 and 14   ....

⑤ 19 and 17   ....

⑥ 11 and 8   ....

⑦ 7 and 12   ....

⑧ 10 and 20   ....

B

Write these numbers in words.

① 6 ....

② 2 ....

③ 10 ....

④ 5 ....

⑤ 1 ....

⑥ 7 ....

⑦ 3 ....

⑧ 4 ....

C

I have these coins.

Colour the sweets I can buy.

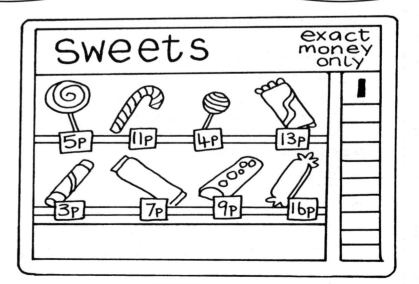

sweets   exact money only

5p   11p   4p   13p

3p   7p   9p   16p

Oral Maths

Ordinals

Ask 5 children to stand at the front of the class in a line.
- Ask questions about the order of the children, such as:

  Who is first / second / third / etc.?

  What colour hair has the second person?

  What is the name of the fifth person? etc.

  Show the children how we write 1st, 2nd, 3rd etc.

- Repeat the game with 10 children or objects placed in an order.

- You will need 10 Ordinal Number Cards (1st – 10th) (see the Resource Guide pages 62–64) and a row of 10 chairs at the front of the class. Ask individual children to place objects on particular chairs according to their position in the line, e.g. *Put teddy on the 6th chair.* Finish by asking children to label the chairs with their ordinal numbers by asking questions such as: *Who can label the chair with teddy on it?*

Use the Ordinal Number Cards, with a washing line and pegs, to carry out the following activities:

- Distribute the cards among the children and invite them to help you assemble the line.
- Ask the children to cover their eyes as you remove a card which they can then identify.
- Swap two cards around and ask the children to spot the change.
- Work with larger ordinals by looking at the position of letters of the alphabet, the position of children in the register, the days of the month, and months of the year.

Mental Workout Unit 20

Adding 11 and 9

Teaching Tips for Set A and C

- Set A: remind the children that adding 9 or 11 means adding 10 and adjusting by 1.
- Set C: draw the children's attention to colour words around the classroom for support.

Answers

A ① 15 ③ 14 ⑤ 20 ⑦ 12

　② 16 ④ 13 ⑥ 15 ⑧ 17

C The aliens should be coloured, in order:

blue, yellow, (blank), red, (blank), (blank), (blank), green, (blank), purple.

A

1. $5 + 10 =$ ....
2. $5 + 11 =$ ....
3. $5 + 9 =$ ....
4. $2 + 11 =$ ....
5. $9 + 11 =$ ....
6. $6 + 9 =$ ....
7. $3 + 9 =$ ....
8. $9 + 8 =$ ....

B

Circle the dominoes which add up to six.

C

1. Colour the 1st alien blue.
2. Colour the 8th alien green.
3. Colour the 2nd alien yellow.
4. Colour the 4th alien red.
5. Colour the 10th alien purple.

Oral Maths

Time: o'clock

- Talk about different times of the day and what might happen at certain times.

- Talk about 'morning', 'afternoon', 'evening', night' and discuss how we need to say '8 o'clock in the morning' or '8 o'clock at night' to be sure the meaning of the time is understood. (Saying 'We'll meet at 9 o'clock on Friday' isn't precise enough.)

Each child needs a Clock Face (see the Resource Guide pages 62–64). Draw four blank clock faces on the board. With the help of the children fill in the numbers for each clock.

- On the first three clocks draw the hands at 2 o'clock, 5 o'clock and 8 o'clock. Ask the children:
  What can you see that is the same on each clock?
  What can you see that is different?
  Answers should include: a long pointer (minute hand) and a short pointer (hour hand), all long hands pointing straight up (avoid saying they point at the 12 as the '12' is for the hour hand not the minute hand), all short hands pointing at different numbers. Tell the children what each clock 'says' and ask them how to show 7 o'clock on the fourth clock.

- Draw or show the children a clock face with different 'o'clock' times and ask them what time it says.

- Ask the children to show you different 'o'clock' times on their clocks.

Mental Workout Unit 21

Number pairs for 10

Teaching Tips for Set A

- Supply Numberlines (see the Resource Guide pages 62–64). Encourage the children to use quick recall of the number pairs for 10.

Answers

A ① 10   ③ 10   ⑤ 5   ⑦ 4   ⑨ 10
   ② 10   ④ 10   ⑥ 9   ⑧ 3   ⑩ 4

B + joins to add, total, sum, count on;
   − joins to subtract, count back, take away.

C ① 6   ③ 6   ⑤ 13
   ② 10   ④ 10   ⑥ 13

A

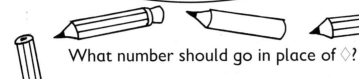

What number should go in place of ◇?

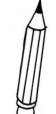

1. $4 + 6 = ◇$ ....
2. $7 + 3 = ◇$ ....
3. $2 + 8 = ◇$ ....
4. $0 + 10 = ◇$ ....
5. $10 - 5 = ◇$ ....

6. $10 - 1 = ◇$ ....
7. $6 + ◇ = 10$ ....
8. $10 - 7 = ◇$ ....
9. $◇ - 8 = 2$ ....
10. $10 - 6 = ◇$ ....

B

Join the words to the correct symbol.

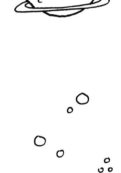

take away   sum   count back   add   count on   total   subtract

$+$ $-$

C

What is the score?

1.  ....
2.  ....
3.  ....

4.  ....
5.  ....
6.  ....

Oral Maths

Place value

Each child needs a set of Number Cards (see the Resource Guide pages 62–64). Revise with the children what the words 'fourteen' and the other 'teens' mean, e.g. 14 means 10 and 4 more or 1 set of ten and 4 units. Discuss the meaning of some other numbers, e.g. 24 means 2 sets of ten and 4 units.

Provide the children with large Digit Cards (see the Resource Guide pages 62–64).

■ Divide the children into groups. In front of each group place two PE hoops. Label the hoops 'tens' and 'units'.
Use one group to demonstrate to the rest of the class how a number such as 21 can be made by a child holding a number 2 standing in the 'tens' hoop and a child holding a number 1 standing in the 'units' hoop.

Now call out a series of two-digit numbers. In each case the groups race to make the numbers by children holding the correct cards standing in the appropriate hoop.

■ Write a two-digit number on the board (up to 30) and ask the children to hold up the card for the number of tens or units for that number:
How many tens in 26? They hold up 2.
How many units in 15? They hold up 5.

■ Continue the game orally so the children do not have the figures to use as a reference.

■ Ask the children to hold up the cards to show the number made by *x* tens and *y* units. *What number is 1 ten and 7 units?* They hold up 1 and 7. Choose a child to say the number out loud.

Mental Workout Unit 22

Missing signs: +, − or =

Teaching Tips for Set A

Explain that each calculation has a sign missing.

Answers

A ① + ③ − ⑤ − ⑦ +
     ② = ④ = ⑥ = ⑧ −

B ① 12 ③ 18 ⑤ 14
     ② 3 ④ 3 ⑥ 0

A

Write the missing signs, +, – or =.

① 5 ☐ 1 = 6

② 10 − 5 ☐ 5

③ 14 ☐ 10 = 4

④ 5 − 2 ☐ 3

⑤ 4 ☐ 2 = 2

⑥ 6 + 4 ☐ 10

⑦ 7 ☐ 3 = 10

⑧ 15 ☐ 8 = 7

B

① ....

② ....

double it

halve it

⑥ ....   take away 6   **6**   add 12   ③ ....

take the number from 20

subtract 3

⑤ ....

④ ....

C

Continue the pattern.

① ....

② ....

③ ....

④ ....

Oral Maths

Bridge 10 with a single digit

- Remind children about the number pairs for 10. Divide a board into two columns, A and B. Tell the children a story about a football match involving teams A and B. It was a very exciting game: 10 goals were scored. Ask the children to think of all the possible results which the game might have had: 4-6, 1-9, 7-3, etc. Record all the results on the board. Encourage children to remember that there are pairs of results, e.g. 4-6 and 6-4.

- Give each child a Digit Card (1–9) (see the Resource Guide pages 62–64). Play a 'musical statues' game. When the music stops the children each find a partner so that together they make 10. Redistribute the cards and play again.

- Introduce a sum such as 7 + 5. Talk to the children about how they might use their knowledge of number pairs for 10 to help them in quickly finding the answer. Talk about how 7 needs 3 to make 10. Borrow 3 from the 5 and the addition becomes 7 + 3 + 2. Since we know 7 + 3 = 10, the sum is now a lot easier.

- Repeat with other calculations.

- Write a series of sums on the board, each one involving the addition of two single-digit numbers and resulting in a total greater than 10. Give each child a set of Digit Cards (1–9). Point to the first digit of each sum in turn. Ask the children to show you what number they would add to it to make 10. For example, in the sum 8 + 5 we need to add 2 to 8 to make 10. Then say to the children, *But we aren't adding 2, we're adding 5, so how many more than 10 will the answer be?* Ask the children to show you this second number (in this example 3).

Use a Numberline to illustrate and reinforce the idea.

Mental Workout Unit 23

Further doubles (to double 10)

Teaching Tips for Set A

- Use dice, dominoes, playing cards and Number Cards (see the Resource Guide pages 62–64) to practise quick recall of doubles and halves to 20.

Answers

A ① 4   ③ 10   ⑤ 18   ⑦ 12
　　② 16   ④ 14   ⑥ 7   ⑧ 9

B ① ◇   ③ ◇   ⑤ ◇
　　② ○   ④ ○   ⑥ ◇

C ① 8, 10 and 14   ② 14 and 8   ③ 10 and 20   ④ 40, 20 and 0

Name	Class	# Unit 23

A

Write the total or put in the missing dots.

① 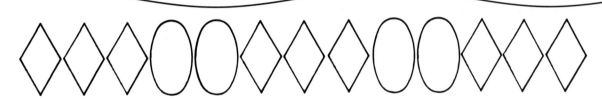 ..... **8** .....

② ....

③ **20**

④ ....

⑤ ....

⑥ ..... **14** .....

⑦ ....

⑧ ..... **18** .....

B

Draw the shapes in this pattern.

① the 2nd shape ....   ④ the tenth shape ....

② the 9th shape ....   ⑤ the first shape ....

③ the 12th shape ....   ⑥ the last shape ....

C

Write the missing numbers.

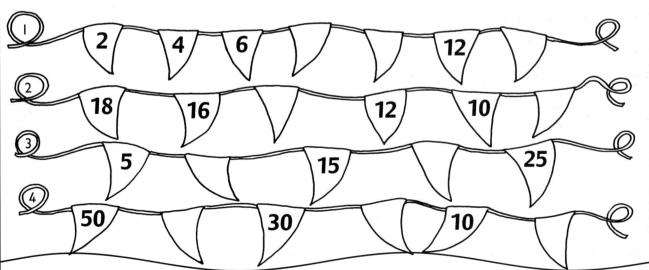

1. **2** **4** **6** **12**
2. **18** **16** **12** **10**
3. **5** **15** **25**
4. **50** **30** **10**

Oral Maths

Time: half past

- Each child needs a clock face (see the Resource Guide pages 62–64) and a small paper circle.

- Start by reminding the children about reading the time for each hour: 3 o'clock, 4 o'clock, etc. Ask the children to show you different 'o'clock' times.

- Ask the children to fold the paper circle in half and and colour one half of the circle. Talk about halves. Ask them to draw a radius along the fold line with a thick dark colour. Get the children to hold the circle as in a picture. Ask them to give the picture a half turn. (Let the children make half turns themselves to see what happens to them.)

  Where is the line pointing now? (Straight down)
  How far around the circle has it gone? (Halfway)

- Ask the children to make their clocks say 2 o'clock. Ask them to give the minute hands a half turn/turn it half way around the clock. (Make sure they move the hand clockwise.)

  Where is the minute hand pointing now? (Straight down. Note: do not say 'at the six'; the 6 is for the hour hand not the minute hand.)
  How far around the circle has it gone? (Halfway)

  Look at the hour hand. (Show the children what happens on a geared clock.)

  Where should the hour hand be pointing now? (Halfway between the 2 and the 3 – ask the children to move it)
  How far has it gone? (Halfway between the two hour numbers)

  Explain we call this time 'half past two' because the minute hand has gone half way around the clock and the hour hand has moved half way to the next number. It is half way past the two.

- Ask the children to show you different 'half past' times.

- Once the children are comfortable with the concept of 'half past', play this game to reinforce the idea. Sit 12 children in a circle, holding Number Cards (1–12) (see the Resource Guide pages 62–64). Explain that the children are numbers on a clock. Now take a long and a short skipping rope or rod and place them in the middle of the circle as hands of the clock. Ask two children to make 'o'clock' and 'half past' times. See how quickly the different pairs of children can work together to show the times.

Mental Workout Unit 24

Tens and units (ones)

Teaching Tips for Set A, B and C

- Set A: remind the children what the 'teen' numbers mean and what 20, 30, etc. mean.
- Set B: explain how subtracting 9 or 11 is the same as subtracting by 10 and adjusting by one.
- Set C: explain what has to be done to the prices of the toys.

Answers

A ① 1   ③ 14   ⑤ 25
   ② 9   ④ 2 and 0   ⑥ 3 and 6

B ① 3   ③ 19   ⑤ 8   ⑦ 5
   ② 6   ④ 15   ⑥ 11   ⑧ 14

C ① £6   ③ £4   ⑤ £2
   ② £5   ④ £3   ⑥ £1

Name _____ Class _____ # Unit 24

A Fill in the boxes.

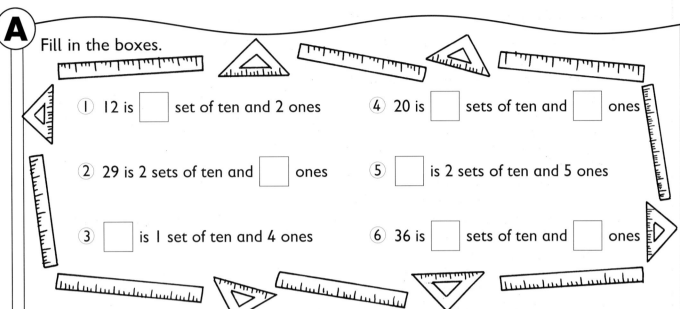

1. 12 is ☐ set of ten and 2 ones

2. 29 is 2 sets of ten and ☐ ones

3. ☐ is 1 set of ten and 4 ones

4. 20 is ☐ sets of ten and ☐ ones

5. ☐ is 2 sets of ten and 5 ones

6. 36 is ☐ sets of ten and ☐ ones

B Write the answers.

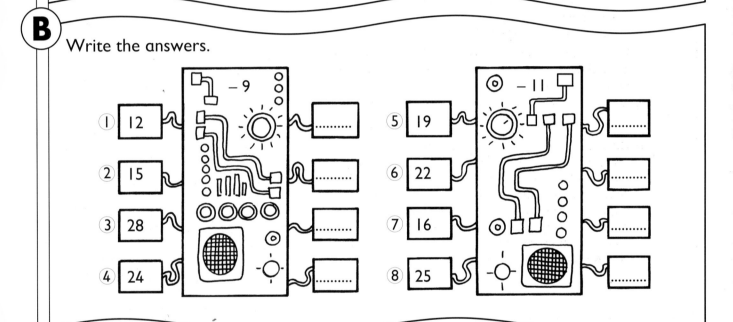

−9

1. 12 → ....
2. 15 → ....
3. 28 → ....
4. 24 → ....

−11

5. 19 → ....
6. 22 → ....
7. 16 → ....
8. 25 → ....

C Write new price tickets for the toys.

Half price sale!

£8 £6 £2
£4 £2
Jigsaw £10 £2

1. £
2. £
3. £
4. £
5. £
6. £

Oral Maths

Patterns with subtraction

■ Look at a number pattern such as: $19 - 1 = 18$
$19 - 2 = 17$
$19 - 3 = 16$
$19 - 4 = 15$, etc.

Discuss what is happening to the number you are taking away and to the 'answer' and why.
(You take away 1 more each time, so you are left with 1 fewer each time.)

Investigate similar patterns:

■ Start with 1 fewer each time and each time take away the same amount.

■ Increase each starting number and subtracting number by 1 (same answer each time).

■ Show how the patterns can be seen on a numberline.

■ Give each child a set of Digit Cards (0–9) (see the Resource Guide pages 62–64). Ask the children to hold hands with children whose numbers are 1 less than theirs and 1 greater than theirs (they are not allowed to link with two identical numbers, e.g. 7–8–7 is not allowed). The children should end up in lines from 0–9.

■ Ask the children to hold hands with children whose numbers are 2 less than theirs and 2 more than theirs. Encourage the children to notice that they have now made lines of odd or even numbers.

Connection between addition and subtraction

■ Use practical examples to show how two groups can be combined in either order to give the same total. Show how subtraction can be thought of as taking part of the group away, or leaving part of the group behind ($9 - 5 = 4$ and $9 - 4 = 5$). Show how three more addition/subtraction sentences can be written down if we know one of them.

■ Show the children (practically or in a picture) an addition or subtraction. Ask them for a number sentence to describe the event.

■ Ask them for the other three related sentences.

■ Encourage the children to check a subtraction by doing the related addition mentally.

Mental Workout Unit 25

O'clock and half past

Teaching Tips for Set A and B

■ Set A: supply clock faces (see the Resource Guide pages 62–64) to support less able children.

■ Set B: encourage the children to 'identify' the number of spots from their patterns, rather than by counting them.

Answers

A ① 5 o'clock   ② half past 10   ③ 2 o'clock   ④ half past 8

Make sure the children put the hour hands in the correct place for 'half past' times (questions 6 and 8).

B ①    **C** ① 1 2 2   ③ 8 8 7   ⑤ 40 5 50
② 1 2 3   ④ 4 14 4

Unit 25

A

What is the time?

①   ③

....

②   ④

....

....

Put the hands on the clocks.

⑤ 9 o'clock   ⑦ 1 o'clock

⑥ half past 4   ⑧ half past 9

B

Colour the dominoes which add up to 10.

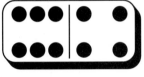

C

Continue the number patterns.

①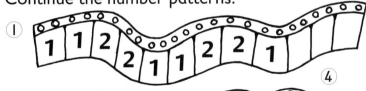
   1 1 2 2 1 1 2 2 1

②
   1 2 3 1 2 3 1 2 3

④
   14 4 14 4 14 4 14 4 14

③   7 7 7 7 8 8 8 7 7 8

⑤
   1 10 2 20 3 30 4

Oral Maths

Bridge 20 with a single digit

- Divide a board into two columns, labelled 'sank' and 'saved'. Tell the children a story about a gang of pirates who stole 20 bags of treasure. Unfortunately some of the bags were lost when their ship sank in a sea battle. Ask the children to think of all the possible numbers of bags which sank and were saved. Record all the results on the board. Encourage children to remember that there are pairs of results, e.g. 14 and 6, and 6 and 14.

- Remind children about the number pairs for 10. 'Notice' how the units (ones) match the number pairs for 10.

- Now introduce a sum such as 17 + 5. Talk to the children about how they might use their knowledge of number pairs for 10 to help them in quickly finding the answer. 7 and 3 make 10, so 17 and 3 make 20. Talk about 'borrowing' 3 from the 5. Write the sum as 17 + 3 + 2.

Since we know 17 + 3 = 20, the sum is now a lot easier.

Write a series of sums on the board, each one involving the addition of a 'teen' and a single-digit number and resulting in a total between 10 and 30. Give each child a set of Digit Cards (1–9) (see the Resource Guide pages 62–64). Point to the first number of each sum in turn. Ask the children to show you what number they would add to it to make 20. For example, in the sum 18 + 5 we need to add 2 to 18 to make 20. Then say to the children, *But we aren't adding 2, we're adding 5, so how many more than 20 will the answer be?* Ask the children to show you this second number (in this example 3).

Use a Numberline, Number strips and counters to illustrate and reinforce bridging 20.

Daily Workout Unit 26

Connection between addition and subtraction

Teaching Tips for Set A and B

- Set A: remind the children of the connection between addition and subtraction.
- Set B: explain that the children need to find the total amount of money in each case.

Answers

A　① and ②　4 + 3 = 7　3 + 4 = 7
　　③ and ④　7 – 4 = 3　7 – 3 = 4
　　⑤ and ⑥　2 + 6 = 8　6 + 2 = 8
　　⑦ and ⑧　8 – 2 = 6　8 – 6 = 2.

B　① 10p　③ 18p　⑤ 20p　⑦ 25p
　　② 13p　④ 9p　⑥ 14p　⑧ £8

C
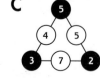

A

Write four number sentences for each set of toys.

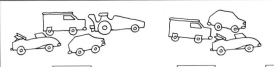

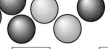

① ☐ + ☐ = ☐

② ☐ + ☐ = ☐

③ ☐ − ☐ = ☐

④ ☐ − ☐ = ☐

⑤ ☐ + ☐ = ☐

⑥ ☐ + ☐ = ☐

⑦ ☐ − ☐ = ☐

⑧ ☐ − ☐ = ☐

B

	I have	I am given	Now I have
①	6p	4p	
②	10p	3p	
③	7p	11p	
④	2p	7p	
⑤	10p	10p	
⑥	5p	9p	
⑦	20p	5p	
⑧	£5	£3	

C

All the sides have to add up to 12. Write the missing numbers.

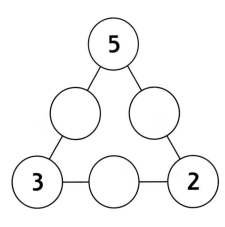

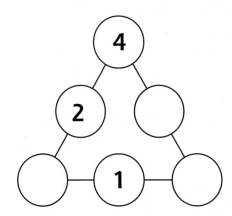

Oral Maths

Days of the week

■ Discuss the names of the days of the week. Talk about things that happen on certain days. Talk about 'today', 'tomorrow' and 'yesterday'. Discuss what we mean by the 'weekend'.

Divide the children into teams of seven, with any additional children divided equally between the groups to act as 'supervisors'. Give each team seven cards with the names of the days of the week.

■ Ask questions seeing which team can respond first by individual children holding up their cards, e.g.:
What day is it today?
What day was it yesterday?
What day is it tomorrow?
What is the day after tomorrow?
What was the day before yesterday?
What day comes after Tuesday?
Which two days are the weekend?

■ Now see which team can be the first to make a week by standing in order.

Use one set of cards to do 'washing line' activities:

■ Distribute the cards and invite the children to help you assemble the line, putting the days in order.

■ Ask the children to cover their eyes as you remove a card, then ask them to identify the missing day.

■ Swap two cards around and ask the children to rearrange them in the correct orders.

Mental Workout Unit 27

Quarters

Teaching Tips for Set A

Remind the children that a quarter is the result of cutting something into *four equal* pieces.

Answers

A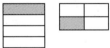

B Half past 7, getting up;
9 o'clock, arriving at school;
1 o'clock, having lunch;
half past 5, watching TV.

C ① 5p ③ 1p ⑤ 10p

A

Tick the pictures which show 'one quarter'.

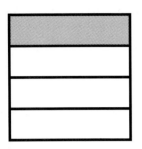
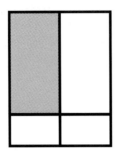
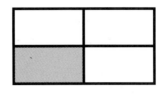
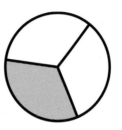
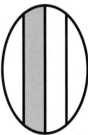

B

Match the pictures to the times.

half past 7

9 o'clock

1 o'clock

half past 5

C

Add one coin to each purse to make 20p.

①   ②   ③

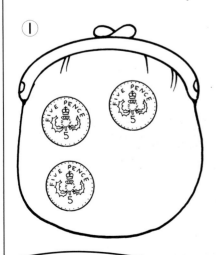
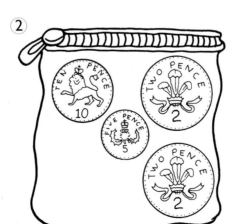
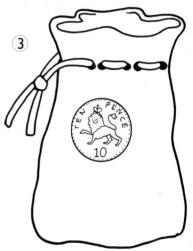

Oral Maths

Counting in threes

■ Each child needs a set of Number Cards (see the Resource Guide pages 62–64) laid out in front of him/her. Use a Numberline and, starting at 0, count with the children every third number. As you count each number the children point to their cards. When you land on '3', they hold up '3'. Continue up to 18, getting the children to hold up the multiples of 3 and then to put them to one side.

Explain what counting in threes means (counting on/adding on three more each time).

Ask the children to read aloud the numbers they have held up.

■ Get the children to come to the front of the class, three at a time and to stand in groups of three. Each time count how many children there are by counting in threes (three; three, six; three, six, nine; etc.). Continue up to 18 children.

■ Play 'slap, slap, clap' (slapping each thigh then clapping) counting together as a class. As a variation, play 'stamp, stamp, clap' as they walk around the room. Play again but this time only say the numbers that go with the clap (the other numbers can be whispered).

■ Give the children a group of objects (between about 7 and 18) to count (e.g. a handful of cubes, pennies, etc.). Arrange the objects in groups of three and count three at a time. They should start by placing the objects on a card or sheet which counts for them.

	3
	6
	12
	15
	18

Mental Workout Unit 28

Addition and subtraction bridging 10 or 20

Teaching Tips for Set A

■ These questions enable the children to use all the strategies they have learnt for addition and subtraction.

Answers

A (1) 7 (3) 19 (5) 28 (7) 11 (9) 21
  (2) 9 (4) 27 (6) 21 (8) 17 (10) 8

B (1) 4p (3) 10p (5) £4 (7) 15p
  (2) 3p (4) 4p (6) 9p (8) 18p

C (1)   (2)   (3)   (4)   (5)

Unit 28

A

Write the answers.

1. 8 – 11 = ...
2. 12 – 3 = ...
3. 25 – 6 = ...
4. 19 + 8 = ...
5. 24 + 4 = ...

6. 16 + 5 = ...
7. 2 + 9 = ...
8. 24 – 7 = ...
9. 13 + 8 = ...
10. 16 – 8 = ...

B

How much change will I get?

	I have	I spend	Change
1	6p	2p	
2	10p	7p	
3	20p	10p	
4	9p	5p	
5	£7	£3	
6	18p	9p	
7	23p	8p	
8	25p	7p	

C

Tick the next picture in the pattern.

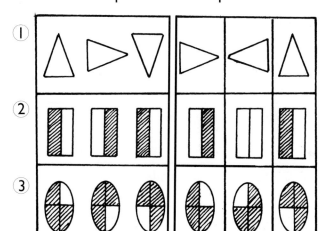
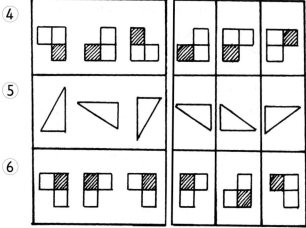

Mental Maths record sheet

	Oral Maths		Mental Workout Set A	
1	Counting on		Counting on	
2	Counting back Numberlines		Counting back	
3	Counting reliably to 20 Extending beyond 20		Match the numbers	
4	In-between		Add 1, 2 or 3	
5	Counting in twos		Subtract 1, 2 or 3	
6	Odd and even		Counting objects	
7	Doubles to 6 Halving to 12		Odd and even	
8	Estimating		Add or subtract 2	
9	Counting on and back within 20 Turning addition sentences around		Add or subtract 1, 2 or 3	
10	Counting in tens		Counting in ones, twos and tens	
11	Partitioning teens		Add or subtract?	
12	Number machines Lazy machines		Addition within 20	
13	Counting in fives		Counting money	
14	Changing number sentences		Number pairs to 4	
15	Doubles and near doubles		Subtraction by counting back	
16	Number pairs for 5 Number pairs for 10		Addition and subtraction within 20	
17	Patterns with addition Revision of doubles and near doubles		Doubles and near doubles	
18	Revision of number pairs for 10 Number pairs for 20		Addition of three numbers	
19	Add 11 and 9		Difference between	
20	Ordinals		Adding 11 and 9	
21	Time: o'clock		Number pairs for 10	
22	Place value		Missing signs: +, − or =	
23	Bridge 10 with a single digit		Further doubles (to double 10)	
24	Time: half past		Tens and units (ones)	
25	Patterns with subtraction Connection between addition and subtraction		O'clock and half past	
26	Bridge 20 with a single digit		Connection between addition and subtraction	
27	Days of the week		Quarters	
28	Counting in threes		Addition and subtraction bridging 10 or 20	

Mental Maths pupil's record sheet

Name

Set Unit	Set A	Set B	Set C	Self-assessment
1				
2				
3				
4				
5				
6				
7				
8				
9				
10				
11				
12				
13				
14				
15				
16				
17				
18				
19				
20				
21				
22				
23				
24				
25				
26				
27				
28				

RESOURCE GUIDE

This is a guide to some of the resources referred to in the ORAL maths activities in this book. You can either make these resources, following the descriptions and illustrations, or they can be ordered from NES Arnold, Ludlow Hill Road, West Bridgford, Nottingham, NG2 6HD, when a catalogue number is supplied at the end of the resource reference.

Numberline

A large wall mounted strip of card bearing the numbers from zero to twenty in a line. This can be home-made or ordered from NES Arnold (Cat. No. NB8509/6) as a Numberlines – Wall set, including: PVC numberlines marked 0–100, 0–20, 0–10 and -10–10.

Number Cards

Twenty cards bearing the numbers from one to twenty. These can be copied from the illustration below or ordered from NES Arnold in three sizes (Cat. No. NB9631/5 Standard, NB9734/3 Large and NB9739/8 Teacher's).

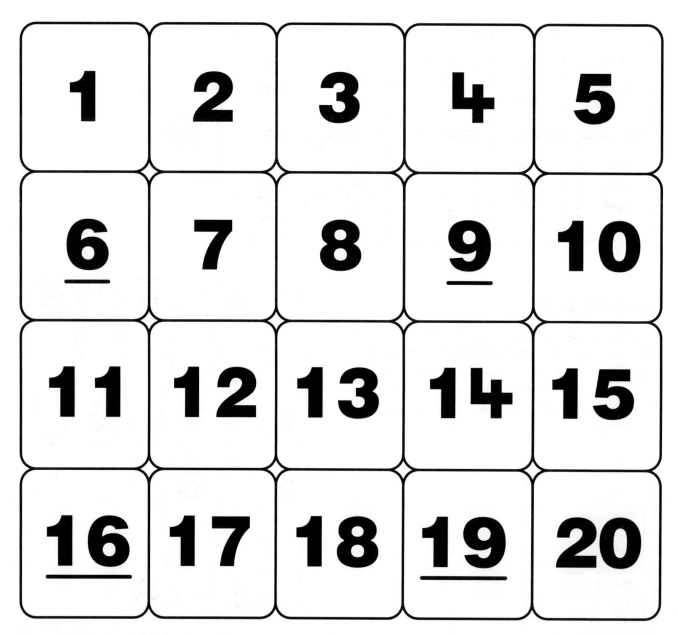

Ele'flip Card

Square of card which can be folded to show any number from 0–10. This can be copied from the illustration (any object can be used i.e. not just elephants), or ordered from NES Arnold (Cat. No. NB8940/4).

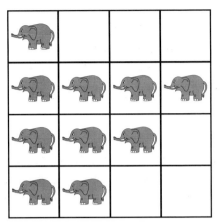

Digit Cards

Two sets of ten cards bearing the numbers from zero to nine and a wild card. These can be copied from the illustration below, or ordered from NES Arnold (Cat. No. NB8941/6 Standard 34 × 48 mm or NB9446/9 Large 48 × 67 mm).

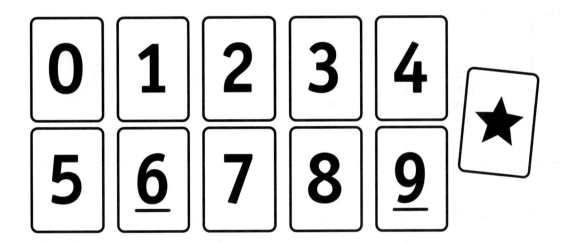

Number Fans

Ten leaves of card bearing the numbers from zero to nine, which are connected at their narrow ends to form a fan. These can be copied from the illustration below or ordered from NES Arnold (Cat. No. NB8974/6).

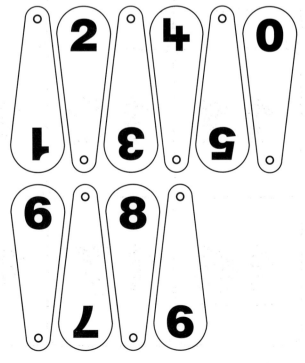

Dice Cards

Six cards marked with one to six dots, as shown on a standard dice.

Ordinal Number Cards

Ten cards marked with the ordinal numbers: 1st, 2nd, 3rd, 4th, 5th, 6th, 7th, 8th, 9th and 10th.

Clock Faces

This is an analogue clockface with moveable hour and minute hands. These can be copied from the illustration below or ordered from NES Arnold (Cat. No. NB7583/1).

Number Strips

Strips of card approximately 30 cm long and 5 cm wide, which have been divided into ten parts and around which elastic bands have been stretched. These cards can be made by stretching an elastic band around a strip of card or ordered from NES Arnold (Cat. No. NB8975/9).

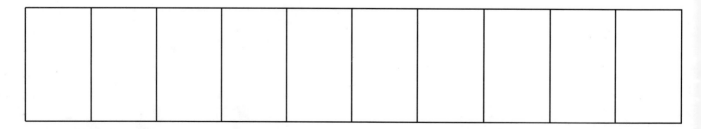